THE FIRST NEW UNIVERSE

HEIDI PRIEBE

THOUGHT CATALOG Books

THOUGHT CATALOG BOOKS

Copyright © 2016 by Heidi Priebe. All rights reserved.

Published by Thought Catalog Books, a division of
The Thought & Expression Co., Williamsburg, Brooklyn.

For general information and submissions:
hello@thoughtcatalog.com.

Founded in 2010, Thought Catalog is a website and imprint dedicated to your ideas and stories.
We publish fiction and non-fiction from emerging and established writers across all genres.

thought.is

Published by Chris Lavergne
Cover photo by Drew Wilson
Art Direction & Design by KJ Parish
Project Managed by Alex Zulauf

ISBN 978-1-945796-13-5

10 9 8 7 6 5 4 3 2 1

Printed in the USA

Gravitation cannot be held responsible for people falling in love. How on earth can you explain in terms of chemistry and physics so important a biological phenomenon as first love?

—ALBERT EINSTEIN

DEDICATION

To the people we were then.

I forgive us.

HERE IS WHAT I KNOW ABOUT PHYSICS

Every time two people fall in love

A new universe springs into existence.

Please do not ask me how I know this, I am not

An astrophysicist or even

Someone who watches the stars

But I've learned through trial and error

That every heart contains a Big Bang

And that love expands outward

At approximately the speed of light.

If you're looking for proof of this phenomenon,

The details are easy to find.

Evidence of every other galaxy

Is hidden in the pages of our history books.

THE FIRST HISTORY LESSON

In the year 2010, every love song that they wrote was about you.

There were no diseases that calendar year,

It never rained,

The murder rate dropped down to zero and the whole world

Grew hazy on the same sweet marijuana high.

In the year 2010, there were no basement floods

Or broken hearts,

No one lost their lives to nuclear airstrikes and everybody

Wanted the same president.

In the year 2010, I found world peace wedged between your floorboards,

We soaked sanctity into your bed sheets

I watched God hand his resignation over and Socrates

Announced a new method.

In the year 2010, the world ceased to revolve around the sun and every wayward planet fell out of its orbit

In the year 2010 you kissed my tired lips back from extinction

And the first new universe was born.

HEIDI PRIEBE

TEMPORARY SPACES

Here's the problem with every boy before you:

They were temporary spaces

That my body rented out by the hour, they were riddles

That we cracked with flesh and bone, spelling

Imagine

What this kind of love might look like

If it stuck around for pancakes in the morning,

Cooing *look*

At this misguided imitation of trust.

The problem

With every boy before you

Was that love seemed to be always running late

Swearing to catch up

Once it sorted through its taxes or

Dropped off its sister at the mall

But it was never arriving, always managing

To navigate improperly and find itself lost

Along the way.

But you,

My heart crash-landed into

With a suitcase full of somedays

I'd been waiting my whole life to unpack.

You,

Love accidentally arrived at

With its compass arrows spinning

And its latitudes and longitudes all crossed.

You,

My trembling body interrupted,

With your hands offering answers

To the questions

I had never thought to ask.

You,

Love booked a one-way ticket to get to,

Cooing *here*

Is where we'll finally unpack.

TABLOIDS

I've found a way to stop gravity's heart and bring extinguished solar systems back into existence

It's called kissing you.

Don't call the papers.

I want to be the only one who's figured out this trick.

GENESIS

In the beginning there were hands,

Tracing electric disasters through my bloodstream.

In the beginning there were words,

Toppling like unattended nations from our lips.

In the beginning there was longing,

Carving droughts into the contours of our bodies, there was

You

Begetting rainstorms with your skin.

In the beginning, we kept miracles

Mounted in the bedroom, we taught sin

To speak the language of our spines.

In the beginning you said

"Let there be peace,"

And we took matches

To the Garden of Eden,

Claiming *this is not the paradise*

For us.

In the beginning, you said

"Let there be love,"

And so it was.

And so it brilliantly, miraculously was.

GHOST STORIES

I kiss you like the summit of Everest

I moderate your body like a drug

You look at me like I am the world's most elaborate magic trick,
wrapped up in your hand-me-down flannel

I touch you like the first day of spring.

You hold me like the lever to a trapdoor

I learn your body like a language without words

You laugh like there is nothing left to look for

We fall in love like two well-meaning ghosts

Searching for houses

that have yet to be haunted.

SECURE BASE

On the first day of the rest of our lives

I took a world map and stuck pins

Inside of each place that I wanted to wake up in,

You said *baby*

We have mountains to climb.

I kept waiting for your mind to request that mine

Stop speeding like a getaway car outside a crime scene

I had grown so accustomed to hearing,

Quiet down

Know your place

Take up less space

But you

Kept on forgetting to suggest that I be

Meeker

Milder

Less

You somehow liked the way

my voice boomed

and my mouth ran

and my wayward affection

never showed up precisely on time.

You said, *I know*

that you're the kind of girl who crash-lands

a little too often

So baby,

I will build you a landing strip

In between my heartbeats, I'll catch you

every time

you fall from the sky

You told me, *Love*,

You don't need calmer waters

or clearer skies, you have a heart

that could outlast any hurricane

And there's no destruction

you and I can't rebuild

into something

absolutely magnanimous.

You said, give me

your plane crashes and shipwrecks,

I will mend them

with my corridors of patience,

I will build us both a home

on solid ground

We'll decorate

with mismatched memories

and unmade beds, we'll live

with the windows wide open

You said *baby*

It's a wild world but you're wilder,

You're a bird

And my heart is a telephone wire.

You told me, *love*,

Go and be free

And so long as you keep coming back to me

I'll be the one to pick you up at the airport

For the rest of your life.

TIME DILATION
(OR, HOW TO MAKE LOVE LAST FOREVER)

It is a Tuesday afternoon

And I've been lying in bed beside you

For ten thousand years.

It turns out love

Travels at the speed of light

And when we make it,

You and I do as well.

(Someone get NASA on the phone

I think I've figured out how to last forever.)

WE ARE FINDING LOVE EVERYWHERE THESE DAYS

In the sidewalk cracks, the phone lines, the street buskers, with songs they wrote for us, always for us. We find love stuffed inside your belt loops, tracing the high wire lines, mapping the six hundred and ninety-four footsteps that it takes to get from my doorstep to yours.

We find love slipped between the couch cushions like lost coins, love growing stale in the refrigerator, love blooming greenly in our neighbor's backyard garden with the shrubs. We turn the TV on and every news reporter tells our story with the daily weather bulletin. Every television show is about us. We accidentally left love in the remote.

Love fills every deep brown freckle of your body, fills your lungs with every halting breath you take. Love creaks out of the floorboards when you crawl in beside me late at night, love hinges between us while we sleep.

There is love crackling like electricity through your bloodstream, love in your Listerine, love filling the steaming cup of coffee that you pass to me over the kitchen table every morning.

We sip on love like an overpriced cocktail, down it hastily like $2 shots. We aren't accustomed to this sudden hit of wealth, dressing ourselves in love's finest garments and flaunting it to all of our friends.

We love like desperate lottery winners these days, not remembering how the windfall happened but determined to cash it in completely before somebody realizes the mistake.

OUR THING IS STRANGE DECLARATIONS OF LOVE

"I love you so much I'm going to crack your rib cage from hugging you so hard."

"I love you so much I'm going to slash my car's tires so that I can never leave your apartment."

"I love you so much I'm going to rip your stupid face off."

"I love you so much I'm going to scream."

"I love you so much we have to break up."

"I love you so much that I'm going to call my family first thing in the morning and tell them that it's over, that's it."

"I love you so much that I'm going to marry and then divorce you, just so I can marry you again."

"I love you so much that I'm going to spend my whole life committing petty crimes so I can meet you down in hell when you croak."

"I love you so much I'm going to rip my whole heart out of my chest and serve it for breakfast tomorrow morning with eggs."

"That's a stupid thing to say."

"I know, I know.

I never get up in time to make breakfast.

But I love you so much that I might.

Just you wait.

Just wait."

SAVIOR COMPLEXES

I've never liked poems about fragility,

Or things that can shatter and break

Here's the truth

about the way that I loved you: It was strong

In a world that was soft,

It was relentless, and goddammit

So was I.

I never wanted any wayward victim complex, give me beating hearts

And hearty bones, your fearfulness

Can rest between my fingertips,

Your yesterdays can sink beneath my skin.

Here is the truth

About the way that I loved you: It was strong enough

To shoulder all of your sadness, it was big enough

To house your whole heart.

Or so I thought back then.

So I thought then.

VINELAND, ONTARIO

A week before the plane-crash dreams begin you tell me,

You are not afraid of anything.

And I have no case for contradiction.

It's easy to be fearless

when you're nineteen years old and the world

is still an open sky before your outstretched wings

I am a bird

And your heart

is the

safest

place

on earth.

The weekend of the vineyards

and the campfires, I tell you

that I don't understand how you and I have not yet been burnt

into the pages of the history books

We've stumbled onto the thing

God must have written

all those sunrises about.

The day before the plane-crash dreams you tell me,

You are not afraid of anything

HEIDI PRIEBE

And how could I possibly explain

That all my real fears I keep clasped close to my rib cage

Like the ways

I cannot find to keep you with me

when the oceans span a thousand miles between us

Like I'm scared

to scour these endless skies without you, like home

is starting to feel more like your heartbeat

than I'm comfortable admitting

to myself.

The last weekend before all of the wreckage

my heart threatens to clip its own wings

What in the wild world could ever feel fiercer

than the touch of your skin on my skin

What if we're standing

on the wrong side of history, braced

to make our greatest mistake

What if your heart is not a telephone wire

And I am not a bird

What if you and I are only two ordinary people

whom all of these metaphors

won't save.

A PARALLEL UNIVERSE, IN WHICH

I hang up the phone

You leave the party

I don't get on the airplane

You drive us both home.

I'm not a bird

You're not afraid

My pride departs me

And your loneliness sits still

You kiss me madly

I love you fiercely

Our hearts stay healed

Our dreams stay wild

You never have to pour your heart out

to the last girl left beside you at the party

And I never have to write you

all of these poems.

HERE'S WHAT YOU NEED TO KNOW ABOUT FRIENDS

Rachel always knew

That she and Ross were on a break.

It just didn't matter.

It turns out love

Doesn't speak the English language

And the only breaks the heart understands

Are the kind that shatter it into

A million

Unrecoverable

Pieces.

WHAT I DO WHEN I FIND OUT ABOUT THE FIRST GIRL

You hang the phone up when I call, so I start running.

Past the library, the rugby field, the roundabout, the highway line, the city limits, the gravel streets, the mountaintops, the ocean depths, the earth.

My body burns. But I cannot stop. Everything inside me is on fire.

I sleep four hours a night. I wake up with anger coursing through me like a shot of adrenaline to my blood.

I go to the doctor and he gives me blue pills. They make me sleep for sixteen hours in a row.

I wake up and the anger's still in me.

I hear the click of your cell phone, hanging up over the thousands of miles.

I hear that click and the hatred boils out of me like venom, like wildfire, like a fury that could corrode the whole universe.

I run so far that Google says my heart might stop.

My heart won't stop. I am too angry to die.

Everything is electric. I'm electric. I am a whole entire ocean of energy, one that can't be quelled or squandered or contained.

I try to run the ocean out of me. I try to drug the ocean out of me. I try to place my head inside my pillow and scream the ocean out of me, but I cannot.

I am drowning in the ocean. It is drowning in me.

I flush the tiny blue pills down the toilet.

I am not faring well at not being in love with you.

HERE IS HOW YOU BREAK YOUR OWN HEART

Stay inside. First just for one day, then two and then four. Turn off your cell phone. Lock your door. Decide you're only interested in what you can control and keep it all between four sturdy walls. Forget to reach out. Forget to grieve. Forget to breathe.

Decide that sex is the answer. Decide that alcohol's the answer. Decide that there is a definitive answer and you can find it. It just lies somewhere outside of yourself. Stay out too late. Wake up too early. Reject every version of yourself that knows you're heading somewhere direly unhealthy. You tried healthy. You are not a fan of where you ended up.

When your heart gets small and quiet, hear its beat. Run your fingers over every tired crack. Then rip it open. Take a jackhammer to all of your virtues. Convince yourself they're weaknesses, not strengths.

Decide that pain's the answer. Decide that self-rejection is the answer. Decide that anger is the answer, and let it take the wheel of your whole life.

Decide that if your heart is going to be broken, it might as well be pulverized completely. Push your limits. Test the waters.

Wonder just how far you can take things.

And then, take them a couple steps further.

THE FIRST BAD MAN

Trigger Warning: Sexual Assault

The first man to take unwanted liberties with my body is also the first man to make me cum

These events are unrelated to each other.

With you I always held on too tightly, worried that if I let go

I would never come back, I grew up deciding on

Conditional love, I didn't understand that coming was not going to equal going

Later on.

With you, I could never let go

With him I let go.

With him I cum and then he takes it

Too

Far.

I stare myself down in the mirror when it's over, eyes glowing electric blue and I know

This is a moment

That separates my timeline in half,

A definitive "before" and an "after" and I'm standing inside of the divide

Holding every multiverse together

I'm crash-landing

with nobody to catch me

So I pick up every scrap of burning metal and I bury it

Inside the strength of my own spine.

I learn how to rely on myself in that bathroom

With the cigarette stains on the ceiling, I learn that

What doesn't kill you

Makes you Angry

And I wear that poison wrapped around my vertebrae

For centuries to come.

No

Was the first word that I learned to say out loud

And it was also the first word to stay lodged inside my throat

In the moment when I needed it the most.

HERE ARE ALL THE PLANE CRASHES I'VE BEEN IN

The first plane crashes into my gym

I don't remember if I'm on it or not, I just remember the engines

Scraping over the rooftop and the wreckage

Lying strewn across the rugby field

The next plane crashes over Hawaii

My cousin warns me of it in a message

But by that point it's already too late,

I remember thinking how much I love that cousin

As the cabin starts to fill up with smoke.

The third crash takes place on November 11th,

The day was meant to be about the veterans

But of course this plane crash has to steal the thunder

From the people who fought hardest in the war

Some crashes I watch from solid ground

Breaking to pieces far above me, tossed

Like ominous confetti

From the sky

HEIDI PRIEBE

Other planes disintegrate around me,

Crooning taunts and unseemly apologies

As they toss themselves glibly

Toward the earth

Years later the hypnotherapist will tell me,

The dreams will stop when you uncurl your fingers,

Breathe the anger out

And let this go

I'll tell her too late, I forgave you years ago

And she'll say *baby*,

He is not the one you need to forgive.

NOVEMBER

It was November and it never stopped raining. I forgot how to begin every poem. There was an undercurrent to everything that season; *forecast today is desperation*

with periods of intermittent rage.

On my way to work I would pen love letters to strangers whose first names I'd never know. *Your hands, your hair, your breath, your scent—another world*

we'll never live in, you and I.

On the eleventh day of unrelenting silence, every future starts to happen in past tense. There are wormholes opening up along the sidewalk and I play hopscotch

with the lives we could have had.

Do you happen to remember that November? You lived fourteen streets, three houses, and one universe over.

I wonder if it was raining there, too.

THE WINTER OF RADIO SILENCE

It's the winter of the drug dealer's basement,

With the blow-up bed, the nightlight, and the hair dryer

that catches on fire.

It's the winter of the odd jobs;

the tattoo shop, the café,

The mall stand

where they sell petrified spiders

Inside glass domes

to odd clientele.

It's the winter of me vowing not to miss you;

With the one-night stands

and cigarettes,

The leases

To bachelor apartments

Where I dye my hair black

Pierce a barbell through my tongue

and wager,

Everything is different since we ended.

Venture,

You wouldn't recognize me now.

It's the winter of a thousand new beginnings,

Road trips

job hunts

blog posts

dive bars

Pennies

Scrounged like tiny heroes

from the couch cushions,

Piling in a jar labeled

"Bigger things,"

(Are coming

I swear)

It's the winter of you walking past the mall stand

With her hand

resting leisurely in yours

And me knowing

that it doesn't matter

How many times I dye my hair

How many folds of skin

I pierce

How many sky-high ambitions

I compile

How many thousands of times

I start all over

You

Are never going to unknow me

And it will always be the winter

Of you being gone.

DISORGANIZED

The way your bones were

The way our bodies broke

The way the river moved

And the alcohol stung

and the night

with its inconsistent endings

The way your Listerine

The way your feet

The way your lips and my apartment and the VIA train

still boarding

two cities over

The way you wanted

The way she was

The way I start missing you so much

mid-sentence

that I forget where to put the rest of the words.

THE STAR-CROSSED LOVERS' CLUB

On the first Christmas without you I decide to have a hot shower and a coffee

every time I feel your absence in my bones.

It doesn't ease the aching

But I *have* been excessively clean and over-caffeinated

Almost every morning since you left.

My best friend tells me I will miss you for a year.

I once heard people are like seasons and you

are the heaviest winter of the century.

I hope you don't come back because there is a tiny brown mole next to your spine

That makes me want to disappear into the infinite depths of not knowing every ripple of your body

like the oxygen filling my lungs.

On the worst days, I pretend that you are lost—

Still trying to reach me but your compass

cannot find magnetic North

And all your latitudes and longitudes are crossed

You are not lost.

You're in some nowhere town, catching fish

and pretending that I never existed.

Good for you.

I miss you in the middle of daytime, with the lights turned on

I wake up with my hands clenched into fists and I don't know

if I am angry at you inside my nightmares

or if my hands are just reaching out to touch you

and then curling back into themselves

because you're not there.

Your absence is an avalanche

resting on my shoulders

Waiting

for us to let it go

Baby,

Let go.

I once flew fifteen hundred miles because I wanted to tell you

It's still you

It turns out love

is just a members-only club that I was trespassing on

for all those years

I watch you love her through the windows of their warehouse

She's a dream but I can pick locks

Like a criminal

And love

has the unforgiving habit

of leaving the back door ajar.

SOMEDAY

Someday we will sit across from one another at a table

With our throats no longer clogged with unsaid words.

Someday you'll say her name and every cell inside me

Won't retreat, looking for somewhere to hide.

Someday I'll run into you at the grocery store and walk away thinking about

Pears and pastrami and kale

Instead of the way it felt to slip

into the hinges of your body

and pray I'd never find my way out.

Someday, you and I will sit

in a well-furnished living room

on a chilly October afternoon

with warm tea and satiated minds

And we will talk

about the ways we thought our lives would go

before we figured all of it out.

Someday I will remember you fondly

As the first, not the only.

Someday anger

will extinguish itself from our bodies and we'll

breathe

without these wildfires in our lungs

Someday this

Will be a nightmare we woke up from

Someday you

Won't wear the only face of love.

YOUR GHOST/ MY GHOST

My ghost sends an email out to your ghost

It says "meet me here" and maps out directions

To the past.

Your ghost RSVPs

Yes.

My ghost shows up two years late

With shorter hair

And sharper bones

My ghost eats tomatoes now

And has its vices under control.

Your ghost

Broke its foot

And got a forearm tattoo.

It has an arts degree now and apologies

Stitched into its skin.

My ghost tells your ghost

I miss you

And puts the weight

of the whole universe

down.

Your ghost heart thumps

like a thunderstorm

beside mine.

Your ghost and my ghost

Sit in silence

For a hundred thousand years.

Your ghost and my ghost

Let the seasons change

Watch the world rearrange

Let all our friends and family members

Die out

Your ghost says

I don't remember

how to love

anyone else.

Your ghost

Sends a calendar invite to my ghost.

It says "Come back

To the land of the living."

My ghost RSVPs

Yes.

THE FIRST LINE

The universe breaks when you come back.

Love beats between us like a war wound or a death sentence

leaving no chance of redemption strung between us

Conscience

plunges its head underwater

and there is nothing left clouding my senses

but your skin

on my skin

on my skin.

Loving you is a trauma

that I do not want the cure for,

stars retreating

cosmos streaking

planets bursting into red and black and grey

Time stops

when your body is with mine

Right and wrong step out for smoke breaks and to shoot up in the living room closet

We're so high

that I'm worried my body will transcend me

It's been years since I have believed in ghosts

And yet here I lie asleep with one each night.

These are the days when I develop an addiction

To the things that are too eager to destroy me, you're the first line of snow-white cocaine, you are the

Thirteenth glass of wine

You are the first false sense of bravado that I'll ever

Illegally inject

You are the first bad habit

that will not die hard

with me tonight.

ATTACHMENT INJURIES

There were days when the sun would shine so brightly that I'd
start to worry something had gone wrong

As though someone had unhinged it from the solar system and
tossed it carelessly out toward the earth

We'd all be sitting in our basements watching pornos

Or taking our Chihuahuas out for walks around Central Park and
suddenly there it would be, the sun,

burning up everything we knew.

We always trusted it to just keep us warm

But maybe the sun had other plans.

Maybe you can never trust a thing that burns that brightly.

THE FIRST INTERGALACTIC TRIAL

As evidence, Your Honor, his smile.

The way it curves into the pitfalls of my conscience

Claiming solace from our greatest mistakes.

If I could call to the witness stand, my senses

They remember it all better than I do

And were once eager accessories to the crime.

If you need a closing argument, my bones

Wrote a confession, they said "loneliness,"

His hands offered a motive, they said "home."

When you're ready to try us, judge and jury,

Please remember that our plea was always guilty

There are some crimes

That are lacking a victim, there are sentences

We'll serve out

For life.

FORGIVENESS

We co-wrote so many poems about forgiveness
Tracing their outlines through the landmine of our bodies,
preaching acceptance with the silence of our skin
You laid apologies out like fancy china
over the dining room table,
Saying "I'm sorry" with over-easy eggs,
I'd preach forgiveness with coffee-breath kisses
We were always apologizing those days,
always trying to come back to each other
"I'm sorry" was an early morning car ride
"I forgive you" was a forehead kiss at night
We spelled forgiveness
with road trips and hotel bills,
Carved redemption with our undressed bodies
in the back seat of your car.

We signed a lease, penning "I'm sorry" at the bottom of the terms,

Signing "forgiveness" beneath the conditions.

We thought that love could be seamlessly reconstructed

With a foundation of endless apologies

Our pasts wiped clean

Our hearts unbroken

Our mistakes

unmade and unaccounted for.

We forgot anger

Is not that easily extinguished

We thought *I'm sorry* meant, "Can we forget this,"

We assumed that forgiveness meant, "Yes."

THE HOUSE ON JAMES STREET

The hardest thing was trying to make the happiness poetry

The pain was always easy; I've penned masterpieces for boys

whose middle names I never mastered, for girls

whose bodies I'd unlearn by three p.m.

I used poetry to stretch between the silences,

to make the voids into something more meaningful,

to force my hippocampus to store things

that were never really there

You were there.

You were there at six in the morning

with the coffee timer beeping

and your body

folded warmly into mine

You were there

at three a.m.

when I would run home drunk and restless,

stripping shoes off and burning feet

against the snow

You were there,

with open hearts and racing thoughts

You were there,

with cold hands and collarbone kisses

You were there

Every time that I was falling,

With a body made of stardust and two lips

leaking infinities

See, the sad poems

only justified the emptiness,

Made the absence into something you'd consider

two drinks in

But real happiness demanded no embellishments

And the truest way

to break a poet's heart

Is to ask about the moments

they have never felt the need to rewrite.

HEROIN

I once read that heroin was like being in the warmest, safest place on earth.

Remember the twin beds that we pushed together on the coldest day of winter in that basement apartment with the multicolored walls?

Remember the steaming pools you'd draw for me in the claw-footed bathtub in the springtime when swine flu arrived?

Remember the candles we'd burn down on the windowsill?

Remember the smell of the river in the spring?

Remember your frigid limbs folding in around mine in April when it wouldn't stop snowing and all of the power lines fell down?

Remember how our bodies produced enough energy to power an entire solar system?

I'm not trying to make light of drug addiction,

I'm just saying that you make me understand

why people inject this kind of thing into their veins.

THE CHALLENGER

It happened every time that we faltered;

The cold ravaging its way through my bloodstream,

Barbed wire spreading like a plague

Around my throat.

It happened every time that I lost you

On the nights when the silence grew too tall,

Our pasts spanning an ocean in between us

My mind always retreating from its depths

It happened every time that I grew desperate

When I needed rain, my fingers starting forest fires

When everyone was starving, I would fast.

It happened sometime when I was too young

To understand it,

This inability to let the world be gentle

The insistence of the minefields

That weren't there.

Growing up I learned brute force

As a primary attack plan

And when I needed love most desperately,

My heart became a city

Armed for war.

ANGER MANAGEMENT

The world was hard

And I wanted to be soft

I didn't want to inherit the anger

that had run for generations down my bloodline,

So I showered off the fury each morning, dressed myself up in cloaks of understanding, hoping it didn't show that hatred

still raged through me like a wildfire

that I couldn't extinguish   .

You made breakfast in bed

and I choked down the smoke

filling my lungs

See, the world was cruel

But I wanted to be kind.

Years later the psychologist would tell me,

"You may spend your whole life waging war

upon imaginary monsters

because you've forgotten how not to fight."

The world was hard

And I wanted to be soft.

I did not want to spend my whole life

Slashing fiercely

at innocuous air

The world was weak

And I wanted to be strong

I wanted only to protect

the things I loved, it's just that sometimes

I couldn't tell

Which monsters were real.

HOW TO BECOME THE GIRL WHO GOES THROUGH HER BOYFRIEND'S TEXTS WHILE HE IS IN THE SHOWER

You come over to talk things out.

You tell me, "I don't want to fight."

We scream so loud I think the anger

might shatter our bones.

After it all

With you sleeping like an angel in my sheets,

I wonder

if I killed every version of myself I could have loved

inside my own twin bed that night.

It doesn't matter.

Right and wrong

seem to have finally overdosed

in the back closet

And consequence

no longer has a home inside our bones.

PACK RAT

I think that everything breaks irreparably eventually

Is that too bleak a thing to express?

On the last day of April I hold our shattered pieces in between my trembling fingers, let the pooling blood remind me,

I'm still here,

Let my arteries continue to convince me,

Broken hearts still beat.

On the first day of May we leave the mattress that we bought together lying by the curbside

at six a.m.

We lock the house behind us; leave it haunted with the people

We did not become

When I was too young to know how or why,

I would collect all of my worn-out belongings

in a heap that flourished under my mattress,

I could never admit that what's gone

Is sometimes just gone, even when you refuse

To let it go

On the sixteenth day of May, I call you

And ask you to come home.

I can't keep sleeping on this bed of jagged glass

Without you in it with me,

On the sixteenth day of May I tell you *baby*,

Come be broken

in my bed sheets

Tonight.

HERE ARE ALL THE THINGS I'VE LEARNED THE HARD WAY

Being skinny won't make you happy

Always watch your alcohol at bars

You can't walk two times as fast as Google Maps

And the solution to credit card debt is not getting another credit card.

Summers can go on too long

Love is a verb

Craigslist is a bad place to find roommates

And being drunk every time doesn't make you any less gay.

You have to splurge on health insurance

No one's going to love you like your Mom

If two things are moving at different speeds, the same thing will happen for them at different times

You can't explain everything with physics.

Time doesn't actually change things

You can't always get what you want

You'll get away with much more than you think you'll get away with, but not everything

You will not be healthy for everyone you love.

HOUSE FIRE

Your heart is a kerosene vault and I am

An accidental arsonist

Lighting fire to everything I touch.

WHAT THEY DON'T TELL YOU ABOUT TOXIC RELATIONSHIPS

I.

No one ever wants to believe

That they are the toxic lover.

No one wants to count the warning signs and red flags and see

"You are here" blinking

inside the summary of every equation.

We're all looking for monsters

Underneath our beds and behind the shower curtains, we don't teach children

To watch for them in mirrors

And in between their bed sheets at night.

II.

When we learn about wilderness survival

We don't talk about the subtle atrocities

That beat their way into our bloodstream, we learn that rattlesnakes and red berries are poisonous but never

how to suck the toxins out of our own system when we realize

the infection lives inside.

III.

Nobody warns you that pain

Makes every red flag look white.

IV.

They do not tell you that each villain

is the hero of his or her own story

because in the real world, no one ever hunts for sport

And the stalker

is almost always more desperate than his kill.

WHAT THEY LEFT OUT OF THE HISTORY BOOKS

It turns out there are some things

love can't conquer.

Most of them

live inside our minds.

KINKS

(OR, "MOM DON'T READ THIS POEM")

You ask me why we don't make love anymore

And *I don't know I don't know I don't know*

I need handcuffs and safe words I need

fantasies and pornographic films, I need to go

somewhere else when you're inside me, I need you to fuck me

as hard as we are hurting

Because I've closed every other window inside of me

through which this pain could possibly escape.

I don't know how to make love

the way we used to,

I've forgotten the recipe

that secret ingredient we had, I have been trying to recreate

Love

for so damn long but the taste

just keeps coming up bitter

So I figured we should try making

something else entirely

instead.

STARS

Your heart is a ghost town

And I am the last patriot left standing

When the dust settles

After the war.

OUR THING WAS RIPPING THE BAND-AID OFF SLOWLY

We do not use our words anymore

But we keep on with the game we've always played.

"I love you so much I'll keep quiet about how you're never in the mood."

"I love you so much I won't comment that you've been staying late each night at work."

"I love you so much I will smile each time I drop you off at the airport, not knowing when you're coming back."

"I love you so much I'll blame the Skype dates we keep missing on the ever-shifting time zones."

"I love you so much I will play dumb when your friends ask why I haven't been around."

"I love you so much I will act like we aren't falling apart at the seams."

"I love you so much I'll pretend that love

is going to be enough to save us."

"I love you so much that it might.

Just you wait.

Just wait."

HERE IS HOW WE'RE GOING TO LAST FOREVER

Two shots of whiskey

Your hands

In the back of the bar, with our hearts

Both boiling over,

Baby,

That's time

So let's outrun it.

You pack the bags, I'll ready the spaceship

We'll stash our senses

In the spaces where the oxygen evades us, I'll conceal you

In the forests of my memory

Where the future

cannot possibly catch up.

Here is how we're going to last forever,

In the shadows

Of our deepest misgivings

With the streetlights writing symphonies

Between us

Your hands,

holding the universe together

on the darkest of nights, we'll get the gods so drunk

they'll fail to notice

That their caged birds

have twisted the bars

and flown free.

Here's how we make love last forever,

Learn the rhythm

of my heartbeat

And we'll sync them

Like misguided criminals

Keeping time,

Baby

I will carry you with me, we'll divide this world and

Conquer,

Meet me every time your eyes close

I am with you

When the silence gets too loud.

Baby, here

Is how we're going to make history

When the floods rise,

And the oceans part between us

Just hold on

I keep spare miracles

brewing on the back burner

You and I

Can rebuild Eden

In the badlands of your body, I'll kiss sin

From the destruction of your skin

Love,

Here's how we're going to find redemption

When the judgment day arrives, tell them

The apple was neither yours nor mine

Tell them

We both watched the serpent walk free

Tell them

We already found heaven,

There is no need

To pass the entrance exam

Tell them, you and I

Intend to last forever

With four trembling hands

And two hearts boiling over

We'll find the way

Baby,

Just trust me

One last time.

HERE IS HOW WE TRY TO HOLD ON

I am holding on too desperately these days,

Baby, I know that.

I know.

I have been trying to preserve you in pieces, as though hearts

could be stacked up like canned goods and stowed away

In case of an emergency, *love*

You were always the escape plan.

Lately I've been lying awake

Trying to burn into the confines of my memory, the way

your smile twitches

and your knuckles crack

and your heart gives like a tidal wave

that has never been warned

of its own strength

It sounds insane, this quiet aching

to preserve you

So I keep the secret

locked inside our silences, I know

that you are holding some there, too

I don't know how we arrived here, me collecting love

like dirty photographs or worn-out sweaters, I was never one

to plan for natural disasters but

lately I am up at night

listening

to the creaking of the rafters

Humming,

Baby,

Don't you feel it?

This storm brewing

inside of our bones?

SOUNDPROOF

There's a room inside my mind

that I have not frequented for years.

The room has soundproof walls and fireproof exits.

It is pristine and devoid

of the racket of everyday living.

There is a room inside my mind that is the

quietest

place

on

earth.

Inside I hear the simplest chambers of my heart

Reverberating alongside my mind, reminding me

The same blood powers us both.

There is a room inside my mind that I cannot always remember
the directions to,

I have spent years

Piling up boxes and shoving excuses in front of its door,

Corridors lined with distractions

Packed with plane tickets

and open bars

and a "90 day fitness craze to get six pack abs!"

The directions to this space are deceptive

None of the compasses point North and X

almost never marks the spot.

There's a room that my heart hates to go to

because inside its walls I know

Exactly who I am

And what I want

And all the ways in which I've disappointed the child

Who once constructed the space.

There is a room inside the quietest chambers of my mind where
I go to be alone

With all the murkiest truths of my own heart.

And in the year

when love starts fading out of us,

I close the door,

I bolt every window,

I lock myself out in the cold

And hide each key.

In the year where our hearts start growing cold, I cannot bear

To hear the soft reverberations,

That the quietest part of me knows,

Whispering

Baby,

It's time to let go.

WHAT IT MEANS TO LOVE THEM ENOUGH

The fifth time that you said you were leaving,

you started sleeping on the dining room floor.

I would sneak in between two and three a.m.,

the floorboards creaking and our hearts buckling under the weight

of all the worlds we had not chosen

and I'd curl in beside you,

pulling crumpled-up love letters from the crevices

of the castles you would make out of sheets.

It all seemed so simple, in the moonlight

with your drowsy arms reaching out around me

and our love letters littering the floor, we could almost pretend

that the universe wasn't unhinging around us,

rearranging while we lay there so still.

I loved you so much that it was fucked up.

And that became a question

that would burn my tongue

for years after you left.

"*It's going well,*" friends would coo over photos of their new significant other. "*We're going on vacation together.*"

"*Right, right,*" I'd want to tell them, "*but is it totally fucked, how much you love them?*"

Did their arrival crash-land your central nervous system;

Endings firing and systems rewiring and the touch

of their hands igniting land mines

through the valleys of your skin?

And when they sleep, is there a universe that stretches

in between their shoulder blades,

Constellations you can map inside their freckles,

and galaxies expanding with each breath?

When they are happy, does the whole world rise to meet them,

like the greatest thaw of springtime taking hold inside their smile

and are you almost too afraid to touch them sometimes,

As though something that brilliant and pure could not possibly
exist in human form,

As though the trace of their skin upon yours

may somehow shatter their fragile other-verse,

crumbling them back into the stardust

they were made of all along?

Do you love them so much that you would promise them

a world you couldn't possibly deliver

And would you sleep on the dining room floor

every evening for the rest of your existence

if you thought that it might make them stay?

And during the coldest of hours

When the springtime in their smile has frosted over,

When the dilapidated remnants of their infamous crash landing
turns to dust and the galaxy that stretches in their rib cage flares
and disappears into darkness

how much are you going to love them then?

Would you swallow their pain like a poison,

letting it sink into your bloodstream, infiltrating the whole of your heart?

And if the winter returned to their smile

and their eyes could no longer meet your gaze,

would you love them still?

Would you recite every love letter you wrote them, begging their extinguished solar system to rebuild itself alongside yours,

or would you pack the letters into a box,

return the cushions to the living room couch,

close the dining room door and let the seasons of their heart

just keep on changing?

I know that you love them *so much*, but what I'm asking you here is a question that I used to ask myself

every morning while the moonlight filtered in around my skin,

creating a prism that I could have stayed frozen forever within,

I know that you love them *so much*

But could you love them enough

To let them go?

GOING, GOING

I think we've both been waiting to hear
Those three little words
That each of us
Is too afraid to say out loud first.
"I'm leaving you."

BLACK HOLES

I keep trying to make brokenness beautiful,

Planting flowers in the cracks between my heartstrings, breathing color into every abyss

I keep telling myself that we can dress all of these failures in kerosene,

And light them off like firecrackers, waging apologies against the night sky

I keep telling myself that we can go back

And try it all again

But here's the only truth:

I miss being whole.

I miss the easy gravitation of innocence

I miss not having to drink and fuck and force myself over

To the other side of darkness

If such a place even exists

I miss not understanding black holes

The way they tear everything near them to pieces,

Claiming dominance over the sky, I once thought

That their antics were malicious

but I'm starting only now to understand

That there are secrets

we cannot handle knowing

There are darknesses

that rip us all to pieces

if we travel too close

because there is no coming out the other side.

There is no coming out the other side.

PUDDLES

Your mind was a storm and my heart
was an umbrella that opened too late.
I'm so, so sorry.

THINGS I DON'T UNDERSTAND ABOUT PHYSICS

I wonder where all of those universes go to die

When two people fall out of love

If they're buried in a graveyard somewhere and whether their tombstones

Have visitation rights.

DEPARTURES LOUNGE

On the last day of the rest of our lives we sleep on an airport floor.

It is cold,

your hands wrapped warm around me and our love

packed up like luggage

to be lost.

On the last day of the rest of our lives we don't fuck

Or make love

Or even kiss

I drink black coffee

I watch your plane take off

And I know

That there is no coming back.

On the last day of the rest of our lives, I have the distinct impression of walking through a house once all the furniture has been packed up and removed

The hallways and corridors and endless empty rooms,

I throw each door open

I run my hands over each wall

I try to find us hidden under trapdoors and floorboard hinges

But we're gone.

There are impressions of us

hollowed into every crease and corner,

Burn marks from our greatest disasters,

Carpets streaked with endless streams of light

We have broken hinges and missing parts, I wonder if we ever fully move out of the houses we build inside of love.

In those days I could still feel you

in the way only people who have been together for a very, very long time can.

"I'm not ready to lock the door yet," I tell you in my mind,

knowing yours is spanning miles

across the ocean

But when you love someone for a very, very long time their mind

becomes a second heartbeat,

pumping in time alongside yours.

And so in my mind you sit with me, on the stoop of that house,

hands reaching over my own,

Friends

In only the way that people who have been together for a very, very long time can be

And you say,

"We don't have to lock it up yet."

And so we sit there, you and I

On the last day of the rest of our lives

And we wait

For the universe to end.

THE LAST LOVE LETTER

I love you so much

that I'm going to let you go

so that you can finally be happy.

.

NEGATIVE SPACE

I know too many women who define themselves by the spaces
they do not take up—the weight they do not carry or the words
they've left unsaid

but I carry it all.

I've spent a lifetime hoisting failures into backpacks,

hustling forward as I pull myself

from ledge to ledge to ledge,

Looking for somewhere

to unpack my ambitions, shouting

"I am here,"

Declaring,

"I matter,"

into void

after void

after void.

I had no patience

For the negative spaces,

Looking only to fill what was empty, aching only to create and invent

But these spaces have been haunting me lately

Pockets of air landing like craters on my skin,

haunting the spaces you used to fit into

Goosebumps rising

To salute your tired ghost.

I never paid tribute

to these negative spaces around me

Until I woke up one morning

and all of them

had filled up with the absence of you.

BEDTIME STORIES

Tell me the story of the life we didn't choose.

The one where we surrendered our ambitions, left our pride out to dry

like dirty laundry and submitted

to the tireless pursuit of one another.

Tell me the stories of the vices

That we never gave into, of the big mistakes

that we never made.

Tell me the version where you didn't kiss those girls,

And I let every plane take off without me.

I like the part

where we're still living in that small apartment

down by the river,

Knees knocking and hearts thumping and all of our lofty dreams

buried deep in the back garden,

instead of regrets.

Tell me again how we stayed strong,

Switching our future plans like seasonal sweaters,

Letting our stories

script and narrate themselves.

I like the plot curve where we learn to spell commitment

Without a second thought or hesitation,

Every happy ending packaging up neatly and thunderstorms

not brewing in our bones.

Tell me again about the actors

that we hired to play us both

How they threw back their heads

and clasped fingers

and made love

like the world was not ending

one innocent moment at a time.

Tell me how summer

never faded from their faces,

How their laugh lines

hunkered grooves into their skin

Tell me the story

about the people who kept loving each other

in all the ways that we couldn't learn to,

Tell me the happy ending

we didn't have.

EDISON

We didn't fail

We just found one thousand ways not to love each other.

The nine hundred and ninety-ninth way turned out to be

Staying together.

(43.557575, -89.245337)

On the first day of September I find the love letters you left in my closet, and I think

This is the worst of it all.

In the fall I walk past the second house we lived in

The one that was blue except now

The bricks are yellow and you're gone.

Two weeks later you bring soup to my apartment when I am sick

And the smell of the back seat of your car carves out a pit inside my stomach

that I crawl into and live in

for the next two months.

You move onto a street that is the same as the last name of the second girl

I'm so sad that every poem I try to write is just a series of disjointed facts

Coordinates, latitude lines, dates

If I didn't know better I'd think

That I was still trying to crack some sort of code

That would lead me right back to your front door.

I FOUND THE PORTAL TO EVERY OTHER UNIVERSE

It is a trapdoor in your memory

Called "Regrets."

I THINK THAT MY BODY'S STILL IN LOVE WITH YOU

I think that our bodies have memories

We cannot access with our minds.

I think our pulses keep the rhythm of sorrow,

That our limbs carry heartaches in their bones

I think our bodies can harbor all our secrets

that our thoughts have long forgotten

And if so, then it's possible my body

Remains in love with yours.

Because the thing is, both our minds forgot so much

Like how to listen, how to compromise, how to be patient and faithful and fair,

We got *so lost*

Inside the noise of trying to love each other *right* that we forgot

how to do it at all,

But I think that the memory is still trapped

Somewhere underneath my skin.

I think the memory of loving you lives on

Inside my fingertips,

They have been tracing the bodies

Of so many other boys, trying to find you,

trying to find their way home, I think my lips

Are still trying to taste you

Inside every other person I kiss.

I think my body is still in love with yours because in the dead of night

When the blinds are drawn and the air is still and someone else's hulking figure lies sleeping beside mine,

It is always still yours I'm reaching out for

When I'm just drowsy enough to not remember

That you have been gone for so long.

They say our bodies regenerate completely

After seven long years,

That all our skin cells

Are shed and replaced

And I hope that isn't true because if so

Then I have six years more to go

Before I finally have a body

That no longer thinks of yours as home.

SEEING OTHER PEOPLE

I get tired trying to write poetry

about anybody other than you.

Every kiss is just another regret

Penciled into present tense

Every body after yours is just a lie

I tell myself to keep warm through the winter

Every time I start thinking "I love you"

About someone else's open heart or hands

I have that dream where the plane is always crashing

and I wake up wanting you to come home.

THE GARDENER

There's a graveyard of mistakes

in my back garden

With your memory

Buried deep inside each plot.

Every morning I sit by its sidelines

Watching for traces of rain

Begging for spring to come again

I've planted

ten thousand seeds

inside your absence

but nothing has grown there yet.

There's a graveyard of mistakes

in my back garden

and the soil won't sprout up anything new

I asked the heavens how to pull through, they said *darling*

You do not belong

Out in the backyard with the dying

There's a hurricane

brewing in your bloodstream

Let the past

bellow and thunderstorm out of you

before a new season can pull through

There's a graveyard of mistakes

in my back garden

and I'm tired of turning up dirt.

I asked the ground

How to make a fresh start and it said

"Baby,

Go and dig up your heart.

Don't you know

that nothing beautiful grows

without a season of rain?"

A LETTER TO THE PEOPLE
WE NEVER BECAME

Yes, I still regret it all. The houses we never moved into, the wedding that we didn't have. I still think about the children with their thunderbolt smiles and wildfire minds, whose parents we did not become. Please tell them I love them when you get the chance.

The way that you loved still leaks out of me. I find it pooling in the center of my rib cage and leaving stains on other people's beds. I'm trying to keep your patience pumping through me, for the days when I am lacking it the most. Every tired mistake still tastes faintly of you. It has been one year and seventeen days and I am forgetting the way you used to look at me like maybe we'd stumbled on magic.

Some days I chalk it up to timing. On my tombstone let them transcribe, "Showed up too late to the life she should have had." That's okay. It wasn't our fault, not at all. We just had all the clocks and the cell phones set wrong. If we could bend time and try it all again, we'd get it right.

And so here's the life I'm left with after all. I bleed our ending into New York City sidewalks, send you postcards from the universe outside. Here is the wilderness of other women's bodies. Here's the lightning storm of other men's minds. Was it worth it at the end of the story? Baby, who can claim to know or tell?

Herein lies the place where our roads diverged. I hope you're happy on that other path you've chosen. I hope you're patient with her inconsistent spirit and you've learned to appreciate his strength.

I hope you know that staying was the wrong choice but that leaving was the wrong choice, too. I hope you know there's no right universe for any of us. There are just an infinite number of mistakes we could have made along the way, and on the loneliest of nights, I envy yours.

On the loneliest nights I write you letters and I know that in some other universe, some alternate version of me is writing back.

We both pay taxes on the lives that we have chosen. And we both sign our surnames with regret.

THE SECRET LANGUAGE
OF LOVERS

At eighteen, we learn love in Morse code.

In the early morning hours when I'm too drowsy to rise, you whisper "Love you" as you steal away to work and I say,

Tap-tap-tap.

My tired fingers reaching out to trace your body, find your center, remind you that *"I love you too,"* even when I'm still half-asleep.

Over the years, our restless fingers become a secret language.

Tap-tap-tap in lecture halls while you and I play footsies under the table.

Tap-tap-tap on the nights when I get home from work at three a.m. and crawl in beside you.

Tap-tap-tap with your arms curled around me after a fight that keeps us up all night.

Never go to bed without saying "I love you," even if our mouths are too stubborn to form words.

Our bodies have a language that our minds were never privy to. Our fingers would forgive each other first.

In the years after you leave I wonder whether I have used up all my love on you.

Maybe we get a finite amount of affection—fifteen hundred shy glances,

Two thousand perfect Sunday mornings,

Ten million utterances of "I love you" that are allowed to mean anything at all.

Maybe you and I just burned too hot, too intensely, for too long

And we used up all our love by twenty-three.

At twenty-four I'm certain that my fingers are all out of forgiveness, that every future love will be a ghost story

before it begins.

The summer of the second bad man, I retire my body completely.

I hang all of my lusts up in the closet, leave my passion lying dormant in the hall.

At twenty-four years old, I douse the fire that once raged throughout my bloodstream and leave my daydreams by the curbside with the trash.

The summer of the second bad man I call you, and we drive out beyond the city limits, because I need to hear the silence

I've evaded for so long.

In the summer where my body is a wasteland, where affection is a drought inside my mind, you lie with me and watch the burnt-out stars above us,

Bar clothes mingling with the ground-soil, all my hopes growing stale

inside the earth.

In the summer when I wonder if I'm out of love forever, you rest your hand against my thigh and you tell me,

Tap-tap-tap.

The summer of the second bad man, I go home and let my tears release every version of myself I've ever had to twist around my vertebrae

just to keep on living in my skin.

It is the summer when I know, without a doubt

That if I used up all the love I had in my life on somebody like you,

It was worth it.

Oh my God,

To have loved you was worth it.

HERE IS HOW YOU HEAL YOUR OWN HEART

You build a home for yourself inside of loneliness. One with closed doors and corridors of regret. Each window gazing out on some other galaxy. Ones where you are happier, stronger, more fulfilled. You stare out of those windows with longing. You look for doors where doors do not exist.

You wake up early. You listen to the rhythm of your pulse. You let it beat all wrong and out of time, *you are still here. You-are-still-here, you-are-still-here.* You stop running when it feels like your heart might stop. You keep it beating, through each chest pain and bruise.

You stop searching for answers to your questions. They aren't locked inside of beer bottles or pills. You smash each window leading to other galaxies and realize they weren't portals after all. They were just pictures that your weary mind constructed. You resign to your spot inside this universe. You let the questions not have answers for a while.

You abandon the house you built in loneliness. You invite people over to your new place, with its dirt-stained carpet and mismatched towels. You stop waiting to be perfect to be loved again. You stop waiting to be perfect to love yourself again.

You stitch your heart together using old needles and inconsistent string. Sometimes the sutures come undone. And so you pick your heart back up and reconstruct it. And so you hope that this time, it heals right.

In the dead of the loneliest nights, your bones still ache. Your mind still races. Your heart still beats in time with a life that you are no longer living.

You do not always heal holistically. You do not always heal efficiently. You do not always find a way to reconstruct your own heart with the sort of surgical precision that protects it from all future wounds.

You do not always heal the way that you'd hoped or had meant to.

But you heal.

Oh *baby,*

But you heal.

PILOTING 101

The takeoff was always the worst of it

Each buckle and shudder of the aircraft

trembling into the sky

So many chances

To fall to our demise, still stretching

In the miles that lay ahead

The ending of the flight

was always nothing

Just an afterthought, a pleasantry,

A celebration of how we didn't burn

As soon as we saw ground, it was over as far as I was concerned

Your knuckles gripped white and mine relaxed on the armrest beside you,

I could fall from this height and survive it

Even crash landings are landings

If you have the will to make it out alive.

If I could go back and take a seat beside us

On the last days of the rest of our lives, I'd say

Sweetheart

Please don't fret over this landing

These are flames

That you are going to outrun.

I wouldn't mourn the earth rushing swiftly toward us,

HEIDI PRIEBE

I would not grip the armrest with trembling hands,

I'd tell myself,

Don't think

about emergency procedures

Just remember,

the way your love took off

Remember every jolt

and every frantic buckle

that you navigated through with shaking hands

Remember

how you eased into the sky, scouring heights

that you were not aware you could rise to

Remember

Every dip

that didn't down you, every storm

that you once glided through with ease

I'd tell us, *love*

Landings are nothing more than tributes

To the miraculous nature

Of a flight

Please don't forget

that for years before you crash-landed,

you soared.

IF I COULD GO BACK, I WOULDN'T TRY TO SAVE OUR SOLAR SYSTEM FROM CRUMBLING

If I could go back I would unlight the candles, return the lingerie, lose the fights, and unfill the silences.

I would rewind the movies, unsend the text messages, forget the indiscretions, and forgive every mistake.

I would tear down the photographs, unmake the beds, hang the phone up, and walk out of every shrink's office.

If I could go back in time I wouldn't bother wasting a moment trying to rescue our universe from crumbling

I would just curl up beside you

And wrap my arms around you while the world ends.

I'd tell you *look*,

I have witnessed the future

I have lived through the end of the world

And what I know now is

None of it matters.

Not the text messages or coffee filters, not the road trips or family reunions or bachelor apartments or brands. Not the betrayals or the suspicions, not the hopes or second chances or other girls.

I'd tell you, baby

Leave the dishes

Lying broken on the kitchen floor, we have to make love

In every moment we still have it.

Let the universe disintegrate around us,

I can think of no better place to let the world end

Than from inside your arms,

Tonight.

HERE IS HOW YOU PACK UP A SOLAR SYSTEM

The week before the plane-crash dreams stop, I go to see you.

You are living at the house that sits on Home Street

Where betrayal never grew in the back garden and

Our love letters never lined the walls.

Your ghost and my ghost

Congregate in the back garden,

Swapping stories and toasting accidentally

To the strangers left to mingle indoors.

My ghost sleeps ten feet

Two doors

And one universe over

From your ghost.

And in the dead of night

When everything goes quiet

I drop the veil of artificial adulthood,

I crawl into the space

where our universe used to be

And I watch the stars go by for a while.

I wonder how often you come here,

If we're ever breathing the same thin

Atmospheric air

Without recognizing one another

I wonder

If you are here right now.

And in the silence of my own imagination, I reach my fingers out and curl them inside

Of yours

An "I was here" sign

Stretching over the galaxies

We used to inhabit

Maybe you'll see it, one night when you need it

Maybe you

Have left one, too.

I like to think

that we can always come back here,

When the atmosphere starts getting too thin

It is the last

temporary space

I will unpack in

And it is the first new universe

whose cemetery plot

I will leave flowers resting next to

for the rest of my life.

EPILOGUE

THE LAW OF CONSERVATION OF ENERGY

(OR, THE FIRST BABY UNIVERSE)

The law of conservation of energy suggests

That in the year 2015

No nations fell

No questions went unanswered

There were zero dogs abandoned in the dog pound

And it was spring for 365 days.

In the year 2015

The ozone layer patched itself together,

Every lottery ticket was a winner

Original sin was recalled by the divinities

And someone finally told the Backstreet Boys why.

In the year 2015

Every criminal was caught red-handed

All the major world religions aligned

Zeus retired his affinity for lightning bolts and Icarus

Grew heat-resistant wings.

In the year 2015

A series of miracles took place

Inside a universe that we will never visit.

See, there are forces

That would rip us both to pieces

If we ever tried to venture too close

But I like to think that light

Comes out of the other side of black holes somewhere

That the physicists were not just idealists

And that nothing created ever disappears completely

Without some equal act of magnificence

To swell up in its place

I like to think that Hawking was right when he coined his theory about

Baby universes,

Born from the other side of black holes

Because light cannot stay trapped

Inside of darkness forever

And baby, neither

Could a love like yours and mine.

The law of conservation of energy suggests that nothing created

Ever ceases to exist

It only ever shifts and changes form

And so here is what I know about physics.

When you pulled out of my driveway

for the last time in 2015

With our failures and a sickly, failing solar system

packed into the back seat of your car

Somewhere else on earth

Some other boy

pulled into a different girl's driveway

With a suitcase full of somedays

He'd been waiting his whole life to unpack.

In the springtime of 2015

As our universe finally flat-lined

A love-struck boy kissed a trembling girl's lips back from extinction

And the first baby universe was born.

ACKNOWLEDGMENTS

Chris, Noelle, KJ and Alex, thank you for the endless faith in my writing and the hard work you put into bringing this book to fruition. Katie, thank you for listening to me talk about black holes all summer. Hawking, thank you for actually knowing things about physics (so that the rest of us can write them into poetry books). Ari, thank you for being both my biggest inspiration and my biggest cheerleader. Heather, Laura and Ben, thank you for being there while I wrote the hardest poems. Mom and Dad, thank you for being the solar systems that I can always, always come home to.

ABOUT THE AUTHOR

Heidi Priebe was born in Ontario, Canada and now lives in Brooklyn, New York. She is the author of two non-fiction books, "The Comprehensive ENFP Survival Guide," and "The Comprehensive INFP Survival Guide." This is her first poetry collection. She is actually quite scared of outer space.

Twitter: twitter.com/heidipriebe1

Instagram: instagram.com/heidipriebe

Facebook: facebook.com/Heidi-Priebe-429367157236598

Website: thoughtcatalog.com/heidi-priebe

ABOUT THE PUBLISHER

Thought Catalog Books is a publishing house owned by The Thought & Expression Company, an independent media group based in Brooklyn, NY. Founded in 2010, we are committed to facilitating thought and expression. We exist to help people become better communicators and listeners in order to engender a more exciting, attentive, and imaginative world.

www.thought.is

www.thoughtcatalog.com.